Kitchen Wit

summersdale

KITCHEN WIT

Copyright © Summersdale Publishers Ltd, 2009
Text contributed by Vicky Edwards
Illustrations by Kath Walker
Reprinted 2010

Summersdale Publishers Ltd
46 West Street
Chichester
West Sussex
PO19 1RP
UK

www.summersdale.com

Printed and bound in Great Britain

ISBN: 978-1-84953-000-2

Disclaimer
Every effort has been made to attribute the quotations in this collection to the correct source. Should there be any omissions or errors in this respect we apologise and shall be pleased to make the appropriate acknowledgements in any future edition.

Substantial discounts on bulk quantities of Summersdale books are available to corporations, professional associations and other organisations. For details telephone Summersdale Publishers on (+44-1243-771107), fax (+44-1243-786300) or email (nicky@ summersdale.com).

Kitchen Wit

Wit

Jane Brook

For Sam and Janet Bakose, proprietors of the stupendous
Crab & Lobster in Sidlesham, West Sussex

Contents

Editor's Note

Home, according to the old adage, is where the heart is. But if one were to enquire as to the *precise* location of this daddy of the vital organs, the kitchen is undoubtedly where you'd find it.

From Shakespeare to modern day celebrity chefs, the kitchen and all that it represents has much to offer by way of memorable words of wit and wisdom. Want to be tickled by saucy sayings on the subject of scoffing? In need of a quote to write in the birthday card of a foodie friend? Fancy a wine-inspired wise crack to accompany your early evening glass of vino? Here, in a carefully compiled menu, you have a veritable feast of funny, inspiring and thought-provoking quotations to choose from; feel free to graze or gorge as befits your personal preference.

May you read and enjoy, remembering as you do the advice of Tolkien: 'If more of us valued food and cheer and song above hoarded gold, it would be a merrier world.'

Bon appétit!

THE FOOD OF LOVE

Cooking is like love.
It should be entered
into with abandon
or not at all.

Harriet Van Horne

Sex is good, but not as good
as fresh, sweet corn.

Garrison Keillor

There is no sight on earth more
appealing than the sight of a woman
making dinner for someone she loves.

Thomas Wolfe

Great food is
like great sex.
The more you have,
the more you want.

Gael Greene

Kissing don't last:
cookery do.

George Meredith

Food has it over sex for variety. Hedonistically, gustatory possibilities are much broader than copulatory ones.

Joseph Epstein

———

Anybody who believes that the way to a man's heart is through his stomach flunked geography.

Robert Byrne

He was healthy right up to
the day he killed himself.

Johnny Carson talking about the man who gave
up smoking, drinking, sex and rich food

———◆———

Forget love, I'd rather
fall in chocolate.

Anonymous

———◆———

Whosoever says 'truffle', utters
a grand word, which awakens
erotic and gastronomic ideas...

Jean Anthelme Brillat-Savarin

There is nothing like good food,
good wine and a bad girl.

Anonymous

My favourite thing in the world is a
box of fine European chocolates
which is, for sure, better than sex.

Alicia Silverstone

There's nothing sexier than a
poached pear with a perfect sorbet.

Lisa Hershey

There are few virtues a man
can possess more erotic
than culinary skill.

Isabel Allende

The right diet directs sexual
energy into the parts that matter.

Barbara Cartland

———

When you get to fifty-two, food
becomes more important than sex.

Tom Lehrer

BREAKFAST, LUNCH AND TEA

Never work before
breakfast; if you
have to work before
breakfast, eat your
breakfast first.

Josh Billings

All happiness
depends on a
leisurely breakfast.

John Gunther

The critical period in
matrimony is breakfast time.

A. P. Herbert

———————

Like dresses that do up at the
back, the English breakfast was
invented as a status symbol.

Robert Morley

Ask not what you can
do for your country.
Ask what's for lunch.

Orson Welles

I've never met a woman in my life
who would give up lunch for sex.

Erma Bombeck

————◆————

I never drink coffee at lunch. I find it
keeps me awake for the afternoon.

Ronald Reagan

————◆————

Luncheon: as much food
as one's hand can hold.

Samuel Johnson, *A Dictionary of
the English Language*

Ecstasy is a glass of tea and a
piece of sugar in the mouth.

Alexander Pushkin

—◆—

I always fear that creation
will expire before teatime.

Sydney Smith

—◆—

If man has no tea in him, he is
incapable of understanding
truth and beauty.

Japanese proverb

Never trust a man who, when left alone in a room with a tea cosy, doesn't try it on.

Billy Connolly

The perfect temperature for tea is two degrees hotter than just right.

Terri Guillemets

Remember the tea kettle. It
is always up to its neck in hot
water, yet it still sings.

Anonymous

Jf you are cold, tea will warm you.
Jf you are too heated, it will cool you.
Jf you are depressed, it will cheer you.
Jf you are excited, it will calm you.

William Gladstone

Tea is drunk to forget
the din of the world.

T'ien Yiheng

Strange how a teapot can
represent at the same time
the comforts of solitude and
the pleasures of company.

Anonymous

COME DINE WITH ME

Music with dinner is
an insult both to the
cook and the violinist.

G. K. Chesterton

Strange to see how a good dinner
and feasting reconciles everybody.

Samuel Pepys

Fervet olla, vivit amicitia.

(While the pot boils, friendship endures.)
Latin proverb

Never serve oysters in a month
that has no pay-cheque in it.

P. J. O'Rourke

If I were invited to
a dinner party with
my characters,
I wouldn't show up.

Theodor 'Dr Seuss' Geisel

The best number for a
dinner party is two – me and
a damn good head waiter.

Nubar Gulbenkian

My doctor told me to stop having
intimate dinner parties for four.
Unless there are three other people.

Orson Welles

A man who can dominate a London dinner table can dominate the world.

Oscar Wilde

One should eat wisely but not too well, and talk well but not too wisely.

W. Somerset Maugham giving advice on dinner parties

Laughter is brightest where food is best.

Irish proverb

BREAD HEADS

How can a nation
be great if its bread
tastes like Kleenex?

Julia Child

The first time I ate organic wholegrain bread I swear it tasted like roofing material.

Robin Williams

❦

... good bread with fresh butter, the greatest of feasts.

James Beard

❦

When you share your last crust of bread with a beggar... you must give humbly.

Giovanni Guareschi

Bread is the king of
the table and all else is
merely the court that
surrounds the king.

Louis Bromfield

I would say to housewives, be
not daunted by one failure, nor
by twenty. Resolve that you
will have good bread, and never
cease striving after this result
till you have effected it.

Marion Cabell Tyree, *Housekeeping in Old Virginia*

Good bread is the great need
in poor homes, and oftentimes
the best appreciated luxury in
the homes of the very rich.

Mrs Nellie Duling Gans, *A Book for a Cook*

There are people in the world so hungry, that God cannot appear to them except in the form of bread.

Mahatma Gandhi

❦

Blues is to jazz what yeast is to bread. Without it, it's flat.

Carmen McRae

❦

If thou tastest a crust of bread, thou tastest all the stars and all the heavens.

Robert Browning

If they can make penicillin out
of mouldy bread, they can sure
make something out of you.

Muhammad Ali

Bread is the warmest, kindest of
all words. Write it always with a
capital letter, like your own name.

Anonymous

POSH NOSH

... having invented
the sublime mystery
of haute cuisine,
he went and gave
it to the French.

A. A. Gill on why God must have
a weird sense of humour

Nouvelle cuisine...
ever less food on
greater expanses
of porcelain at
increasing prices.

Sir Clement Freud

Caviar is to dining what a sable coat is to a girl in evening dress.

Ludwig Bemelmans

I never see any home cooking. All I get is fancy stuff.

Prince Phillip

It has nothing to do with frogs' legs. No amphibian is harmed in the making of this dish.

Nigella Lawson explaining toad-in-the-hole to Americans

Boiled mutton is pretty poor stuff
to a man with caviar memories.

Groucho Marx

———◆———

Cuisine is only about making
foods taste the way they
are supposed to taste.

Charlie Trotter

———◆———

They call for dates and
quinces in the pastry.

William Shakespeare, *Romeo and Juliet*

A woman should never be seen
eating or drinking, unless it be lobster
salad and champagne, the only true
feminine and becoming friends.

Lord Byron

Life's too short to stuff a mushroom.

Shirley Conran

Cooks do meals for people
they know and love. Chefs
do it anonymously for anyone
who has the price.

A. A. Gill on the difference between chefs and cooks

Cuisine is just fine,
but there are times
when food is better.

Anonymous

KITCHEN CAPRICE

If you can't stand
the heat, get out
of the kitchen.

Harry S. Truman

The feminist movement has
helped open minds and kitchens
to the notion that men can
be at home on the range.

René Veaux

In large states, public education
will always be mediocre, for the
same reason that in large kitchens
the cooking is usually bad.

Friedrich Nietzsche

A man who loves good food
has a way of making it gravitate
toward his kitchen.

Angelo Pellegrini, *The Unprejudiced Palate*

A good kitchen should be
sufficiently remote from the principal
apartments of the house, that the
members, visitors, or guests of the
family, may not perceive the odour
incident to cooking, or hear the
noise of culinary operations.

Mrs Beeton, *Book of Household Management*

We owe much to the fruitful
meditation of our sages, but
a sane view of life is, after all,
elaborated mainly in the kitchen.

Joseph Conrad

———————

I don't like to say that my kitchen
is a religious place, but I would say
that if I were a voodoo priestess,
I would conduct my rituals there.

Pearl Bailey

A messy kitchen is a happy kitchen
and this kitchen is delirious.

Anonymous

When I'm old and grey, I want to
have a house by the sea. And paint.
With a lot of wonderful chums, good
music and booze around. And a
damn good kitchen to cook in.

Ava Gardner

The kitchen is a
country in which there
are always discoveries
to be made.

Grimod de la Reynière

RECIPES FOR DISASTER
AND DELICIOUSNESS

Don't cook steaks
in the toaster,
even little ones.

P. J. O'Rourke

... Like The Thing That Ate
Fulham. Or the Thing That
Fulham Wouldn't Eat, more like.

**Billy Connolly on the appearance of
some of his culinary efforts**

As everybody knows, there is
only one infallible recipe for the
perfect omelette: your own.

Elizabeth David

I think the hippest ingredient
right now is nostalgia.

Nigel Slater

Recipe: a series of step-by-step instructions for preparing ingredients you forgot to buy, in utensils you don't own, to make a dish the dog wouldn't eat.

Anonymous

———•———

Beware the term 'local delicacy'. It's usually code for something revolting.

Lillian Marsano

———•———

A recipe is only a theme, which an intelligent cook can play each time.

Madame Benoît

GLUTTONY AND GORGING

A lot of vices are secret but not gluttony – it shows. It certainly shows on me.

Orson Welles

He hath eaten me
out of house and
home; he hath put all
my substance into
that fat belly of his.

William Shakespeare, *Henry IV Part I*

Part of the secret of success in
life is to eat what you like and
let the food fight it out inside.

Mark Twain

Let your head be more than
a funnel to your stomach.

German proverb

A gourmet is just a
glutton with brains.

Phillip W. Haberman Jr

A man who has dined satisfactorily
experiences a yearning love
towards all his fellow-creatures...
for the moment, he does not
even hate his wife's relations.

Jerome K. Jerome

A gourmet who thinks of calories is
like a tart who looks at her watch.

James Beard

... everything I don't eat has been proved to be indispensable for life. But I go marching on.

George Bernard Shaw

I have left many things unfinished in my life, but never a bar of chocolate.

Robert Morley

Nothing would be more tiresome than eating and drinking if God had not made them a pleasure as well as a necessity.

Voltaire

Great eaters and great
sleepers are incapable of
anything else that is great.

Henry IV of France

If more of us valued food and
cheer and song above hoarded
gold, it would be a merrier world.

J. R. R. Tolkien

RAISING A GLASS

When I read about
the evils of drinking,
I gave up reading.

Henny Youngman

Beer is a wholesome liquor... it abounds with nourishment.

Dr Benjamin Rush

I like my whisky old and my women young.

Errol Flynn

My rule of life prescribed as an absolutely sacred rite smoking cigars and also the drinking of alcohol before, after and if need be during all meals and in the intervals between them.

Winston Churchill

One Martini is all right. Two are too many, and three are not enough.

James Thurber

———

You are not drunk if you can lie on the floor without holding on.

Dean Martin

What two ideas are more inseparable
than Beer and Britannia?

Sydney Smith

❖

The light music of whiskey falling
into a glass – an agreeable interlude.

James Joyce

❖

I should never have switched
from Scotch to Martinis.

Humphrey Bogart's last words

Why, sir, for my part
I say the gentleman
had drunk himself out
of his five senses.

William Shakespeare, *The Merry Wives of Windsor*

Beer: take pure spring water.
The finest grains. The richest
ingredients. And then run
them through a horse.

Anonymous

Why don't you get out of that
wet coat and into a dry Martini?

Robert Benchley

Vodka is tasteless going down,
but it is memorable coming up.

Garrison Keillor

I'm not a heavy drinker, I can sometimes go for hours without touching a drop.

Noel Coward

❦

Rum, n: generically, fiery liquors that produce madness in total abstainers.

Ambrose Bierce

If you keep on drinking rum,
the world will soon be quit of
a very dirty scoundrel.

Robert Louis Stevenson

Passing the vodka bottle.

Keith Richards on how he keeps in shape

I never drink anything stronger
than gin before breakfast

W. C. Fields

He was a wise man who
invented beer.

Plato

All the great villainies of history,
from the murder of Abel to the
Treaty of Versailles, have been
perpetuated by sober men,
and chiefly by teetotallers.

H. L. Mencken

Always do sober what you said you'd do when you were drunk. That will teach you to keep your mouth shut!

Charles Scribner Jr

DINING OUT

The secret of a
successful restaurant
is sharp knives.

George Orwell

He spends a lot of time in restaurant kitchens and usually has strong opinions about them.

Bryan Miller on why the dishwasher repairman is the best person to recommend a good restaurant

———•———

There is no point in going to them if one intends to keep one's belt buckled.

Frederic Raphael on why great restaurants are like brothels

A kind of living fantasy in which diners are the most important members of the cast.

Warner LeRoy's definition of a restaurant

There are two things you should avoid approaching from the rear: restaurants and horses.

Evelyn Waugh

The disparity between a restaurant's price and food quality rises in direct proportion to the size of the pepper mill.

Bryan Miller

It's so beautifully arranged on the plate – you know someone's fingers have been all over it.

Julia Child

Look here, Steward, if this is coffee, I want tea; but if this is tea, then I wish for coffee.

Punch

SOUPER DOOPER

Good manners:
the noise you don't
make when you're
eating soup.

Bennett Cerf

Soup puts the heart at ease,
calms down the violence of hunger,
eliminates the tension of the day, and
awakens and refines the appetite.

Auguste Escoffier

I live on good soup, not
on fine words.

Molière

I believe I once considerably
scandalised her by declaring that
clear soup was a more important
factor in life than a clear conscience.

Saki

Having a good wife and rich
cabbage soup, seek not other things.

Russian proverb

To feel safe and
warm on a cold wet
night, all you really
need is soup.

Laurie Colwin

There was a Young Lady of Poole,
Whose soup was excessively cool;
So she put it to boil,
By the aid of some oil,
That ingenious Young
Lady of Poole.

Edward Lear

Only the pure of heart
can make good soup.

Ludwig van Beethoven

Soup and fish explain half
the emotions of human life.

Sydney Smith

Of all the items on the menu,
soup is that which exacts the
most delicate perfection and
the strictest attention.

Auguste Escoffier

Hot soup at table is very vulgar; it either leads to an unseemly mode of taking it, or keeps people waiting too long whilst it cools. Soup should be brought to table only moderately warm.

Charles Day, *Hints on Etiquette*

POOH! IS THAT YOU?

Fish is the only food
that is considered
spoiled once it smells
like what it is.

P. J. O'Rourke

A nickel will get
you on the subway,
but garlic will get
you a seat.

New York proverb

For unknown foods the nose acts always as a sentinel and cries, 'Who goes there?'

Jean Anthelme Brillat-Savarin

And, most dear actors, eat no onions or garlic, for we are to utter sweet breath; and I do not doubt but to hear them say, it is a sweet comedy.

William Shakespeare, *A Midsummer Night's Dream*

There are five elements:
earth, air, fire and garlic.

Louis Diat

———

Oh, that miracle clove! Not only
does garlic taste good, it cures
baldness and tennis elbow, too.

Laurie Burrows Grad

———

Garlick maketh a man wynke,
drynke and stynke.

Thomas Nash

There is no such thing
as a little garlic.

Anonymous

***

Presently, we were aware of an
odour gradually coming towards us,
something musky, fiery, savoury,
mysterious, a hot drowsy smell, that
lulls the senses, and yet enflames
them; the truffles were coming.

William Makepeace Thackeray

***

Mine eyes smell onions;
I shall weep anon.

William Shakespeare, *All's Well That Ends Well*

Hallo! A great deal of steam! The pudding of the copper. A smell like a washing-day! That was the cloth. A smell like an eating-house and a pastrycook's next door to each other, with a laundress's next door to that. That was the pudding.

Charles Dickens, *A Christmas Carol*

Much more of Garlick would be used for its wholesomeness, were it not for the offensive smell it gives to the by-standers.

John Woolridge, *The Art of Gardening*

HARD TO SWALLOW

I will not eat oysters.
I want my food
dead – not sick, not
wounded – dead.

Woody Allen

I'm frightened of eggs, worse
than frightened, they revolt me.

Alfred Hitchcock

... made out of frozen glops of
pig fat, soya beans and fish oil.

Peter Cook on his suspicions regarding
the ingredients of ice cream

Sorry, I don't do offal.

Jamie Oliver when invited to help improve
food in the Westminster kitchens

Truly, thou art damned like an
ill roasted egg, all on one side.

William Shakespeare, *As You Like It*

❧

Nobody who isn't an otter has
ever eaten two whelks at a sitting.

A. A. Gill

❧

In Mexico we have a word
for sushi – bait.

José Simon

I am a lifelong enemy of tapioca.

Robert Morley

He was a bold man who first
swallowed an oyster.

James I of England

Unquiet meals make ill digestions.

William Shakespeare, *The Comedy of Errors*

There was an old person who sung,
Bloo – Sausages!
Kidnies! and Tongue!
Bloo! Bloo! my dear Madam,
My name is Old Adam.
Bloo! Sausages – Kidnies,
and Tongue!

Edward Lear

What is food to one, is to
others bitter poison.

Lucretius

Nothing seems to please a fly so much as to be taken for a currant, and if it can be baked in a cake and palmed off on the unwary, it dies happy.

Mark Twain

VEG OUT

Shipping is a
terrible thing to
do to vegetables.
They probably
get jet-lagged,
just like people.

Elizabeth Berry

Large, naked, raw carrots
are acceptable as food only
to those who lie in hutches
eagerly awaiting Easter.

Fran Lebowitz

Nothing will benefit human
health and increase chances of
survival on Earth as much as the
evolution to a vegetarian diet.

Albert Einstein

Vegetables are the food of the earth; fruit seems more the food of the heavens.

Sepal Felicivant

Training is everything. The peach was once a bitter almond; cauliflower is nothing but cabbage with a college education.

Mark Twain

Life expectancy would grow by leaps and bounds if green vegetables smelled as good as bacon.

Doug Larson

Welcome to the Church of the
Holy Cabbage. Lettuce pray.

Anonymous

———◆———

The greatest delight the fields and
woods minister is the suggestion
of an occult relation between
man and the vegetable. I am not
alone and unacknowledged.
They nod to me and I to them.

Ralph Waldo Emerson

Vegetarianism is harmless enough,
though it is apt to fill a man with
wind and self-righteousness.

Robert Hutchinson

❧

They are the Devil's vegetable.

Captain Wayne Keble banning Brussels
sprouts from warship *HMS Bulwark*

❧

Vegetarians have wicked,
shifty eyes, and laugh in a
cold, calculating manner.

J. B. Morton

I'm President of the United States and I'm not going to eat any more broccoli!

George Bush

SMALL APPETITES

I like children.
If they're properly
cooked.

W. C. Fields

Children should come to the
table clean and in a merry mood.

Erasmus

As a rule, children dislike foods
which are said to be good for them,
or are forced on them, and they take
strong fancies to foods which they
are not allowed to eat; advantage
should be taken of these tendencies.

Eric Pritchard, *Infant Education*

My children won't
eat my food. If it is
not plastic or out
of a box, then they
are not interested.

Nigella Lawson

As a child my family's menu
consisted of two choices:
take it or leave it.

Buddy Hackett

***

Even when freshly washed and
relieved of all obvious confections,
children tend to be sticky.

Fran Lebowitz

***

Many kids can tell you about
drugs but do not know what
celery or courgettes taste like.

Jamie Oliver

... making my brother laugh so hard that food came out of his nose.

Garrison Keillor recalling childhood high spots

A food is not necessarily essential just because your child hates it.

Katherine Whitehorn

What is patriotism but the love of the food one ate as a child?

Lin Yutang

HAVE YOUR CAKE
AND EAT IT

Be sweet and honest
always, but for
God's sake don't
eat my doughnuts!

Emma Bunton

Hell is a cake with no icing.

Anonymous

—•—

Dost thou think because
thou art virtuous there shall
be no more cakes and ale?

William Shakespeare, *Twelfth Night*

—•—

Let them eat cake.

Marie Antoinette

There was an Old Person of Rheims,
Who was troubled with horrible dreams;
So, to keep him awake, they fed him with cake,
Which amused that Old Person of Rheims.

Edward Lear

A cake is a very good
test of an oven.

Delia Smith

A geological homemade cake.

Charles Dickens on fruitcake

A compromise is the art of dividing
a cake in such a way that everyone
believes he has the biggest piece.

Ludwig Erhard

The most dangerous
food is wedding cake.

James Thurber

By the way, we never eat anyone's
health, always drink it. Why should
we not stand up now and then and
eat a tart to somebody's success?

Jerome K. Jerome

WORLD CUISINE

Chopsticks are
one of the reasons
the Chinese never
invented custard.

Spike Milligan

The trouble with eating Italian food is that five or six days later you're hungry again.

George Miller

I'll bet what motivated the
British to colonise so much of
the world is that they were just
looking for a decent meal.

Martha Harrison

A nickel's worth of goulash beats
a five-dollar can of vitamins.

Martin H. Fischer

You can find your way across
this country using burger joints
the way a navigator uses stars.

Charles Kuralt

The army from Asia introduced a foreign luxury to Rome; it was then the meals began to require more dishes and more expenditure.

Titus Livius, *The Annals of Imperial Rome*

All you see, I owe to spaghetti.

Sophia Loren

I don't think America will have really made it until we have our own salad dressing. Until then we're stuck behind the French, Italians, Russians and Caesarians.

Pat McNelis

COOKING UP A STORM

When baking, follow
directions. When
cooking, go by
your own taste.

Laiko Bahrs

Cookery has become a noble art, a noble science; cooks are gentlemen.

Robert Burton

'Tis an ill cook that cannot lick his own fingers.

William Shakespeare, *Romeo and Juliet*

If cooking is an art, I think we're in our Dada phase.

David Sedaris

Swearing is industry
language. For as
long as we're alive
it's not going to
change. You've got
to be boisterous
to get results.

Gordon Ramsay

Football and cookery are
the two most important
subjects in this country.

Delia Smith

❖

An empty belly is the best cook.

Estonian proverb

❖

Cooking is a minor art. I can't
imagine an hilarious soufflé,
or a deeply moving stew.

Kenneth Tynan

A well made sauce will make even an elephant or a grandfather palatable.

Grimod de la Reynière

The discovery of a new dish does more for the happiness of mankind than the discovery of a new star.

Jean Anthelme Brillat-Savarin

I maintain standards and I strive for perfection. That level of pressure is conveyed in a very bullish way and that's what cooking is all about.

Gordon Ramsay

A good cook is a peculiar gift of the gods. From the brain to the palate, from the palate to the finger's end.

Walter Savage Landor

EVERYONE'S A CRITIC

When I ask for a
watercress sandwich,
I do not mean a
loaf with a field in
the middle of it.

Oscar Wilde

I hate carrots. Besides, I'm a
boy, not a bat. I don't *need* to
be able to see in the dark.

A six-year-old making a valid point
about not eating carrots

I went to dine at the restaurateur's
place... one is treated well there
but has to pay dearly for it.

Denis Diderot referring to
M. Boulanger's, the first restaurant

If the soup had been as warm as
the wine, if the wine had been as
old as the turkey, if the turkey
had had a breast like the maid, it
would have been a swell dinner.

Duncan Hines

If you don't like my approach you are
welcome to go down to McDonald's.

Keith Floyd

GONE FISHING

The salmon are
striking back.

The Queen Mother when choking on a fish bone

Fish and guests stink in three days.

Benjamin Franklin, *Poor Richard's Almanac*

———◆———

Fish, to taste right, must swim three times – in water, in butter and in wine.

Polish proverb

———◆———

Govern a family as you would cook a small fish – very gently.

Chinese proverb

In the hands of an able cook,
fish can become an inexhaustible
source of perpetual delight.

Jean Anthelme Brillat-Savarin

———•———

'Carpe diem' does not
mean 'fish of the day'.

Anonymous

———•———

... nothing can more effectually
destroy the appetite, or disgrace
the cook, than fish sent to table
imperfectly cleaned. Handle it
lightly, and never throw it roughly
about, so as to bruise it.

Eliza Acton *Modern Cookery for Private Families*

TABLE MANNERS

On the Continent
people have good
food; in England
people have good
table manners.

George Mikes

It is a great breach
of etiquette when
your fingers are dirty
and greasy, to bring
them to your mouth
in order to lick them,
or to clean them on
your jacket. It would
be more decent to
use the tablecloth.

Erasmus

Never allow butter, soup or other
food to remain on your whiskers.
Use the napkin frequently.
Never hesitate to take the last
piece of bread or the last cake;
there are probably more.

Thomas E. Hill, *Hill's Manual of
Social and Business Forms*

Table manners are for people
who have nothing better to do.

David Byrne

Do not move back and forth on your chair. Doing so gives the impression of constantly breaking, or trying to break, wind.

Erasmus

Being set at the table, scratch not thyself, and take thou heed as much as thou canst not to spit, cough and blow at thy nose; but if it be needful, do it dexterously, without much noise, turning thy face sidelong.

Francis Hawkins

PICNIC PITH AND BBQ BANTER

One compensation
of old age is that
it excuses you
from picnics.

William Feather

Give me books, French wine, fruit, fine weather and a little music played out of doors by somebody I do not know.

John Keats

Settlers arrive on great unspoiled continent, discover wondrous riches, set them on fire and eat them.

Vince Staten

That outdoor
grilling is a manly
pursuit has long been
beyond question.

William Geist

Tea to the English is
really a picnic indoors.

Alice Walker

If the rain spoils our picnic, but
saves a farmer's crop, who are
we to say it shouldn't rain?

Tom Barrett

I love being in front of an
audience. It's so stimulating.
I also love to barbecue.

Carmen Electra

THE GRAPES OF SLOSHED

For when the wine
is in, the wit is out.

Thomas Becon

Good God! I've never drunk
a vintage that starts with
a number two before.

Nicholas Soames

I pray you, do not fall in love with me,
For I am falser than vows made in wine.

William Shakespeare, *As You Like It*

Good wine is a necessity
of life for me.

Thomas Jefferson

I am drinking the stars!

Dom Pérignon on his first sip of champagne

* * *

Give strong drink unto him that is ready to perish, and wine unto those that be of heavy hearts. Let him drink, and forget his poverty, and remember his misery no more.

The Bible, Proverbs 31:6

* * *

Go fetch to me a pint o' wine,
An' fill it in a silver tassie.

Robert Burns

Good wine is a good familiar
creature, if it be well used.

William Shakespeare, *Othello*

In victory, you deserve champagne,
in defeat, you need it.

Napoleon Bonaparte

Champagne for our real friends
and real pain for our sham friends!

Anonymous

For a bad night, a mattress of wine.

Spanish proverb

❧

... the healthiest and most
health-giving of drinks.

Louis Pasteur on wine

❧

A man cannot make him laugh – but
that's no marvel; he drinks no wine.

William Shakespeare, *Henry IV Part II*

CHIPS WITH EVERYTHING

We live in an age
when pizza gets to
your home before
the police.

Jeff Arder

We think fast food is equivalent to pornography, nutritionally speaking.

Steve Elbert

Chemicals, n: noxious substances from which modern foods are made.

Anonymous

Pizza for breakfast is one of the great examples of bachelor freedom.

P. J. O'Rourke

It requires a certain
kind of mind to
see beauty in a
hamburger bun.

Ray Kroc, creator of the McDonald's franchise

Why bother to cook TV
dinners? I suck on them frozen.

Woody Allen

If junk food is the devil, then a
sweet orange is as scripture.

Audrey Foris

Oil and potatoes both grow
underground so French
fries may have eventually
produced themselves.

A. J. Esther

Believe it or not, Americans
eat 75 acres of pizza a day.

Boyd Matson

———◆———

Americans can eat garbage,
provided you sprinkle it liberally
with ketchup, mustard, chilli
sauce, Tabasco sauce...

Henry Miller

DIETING DILEMMAS

My advice if you
insist on slimming: eat
as much as you like
~ just don't swallow it.

Harry Secombe

Vegetables are a must on a diet.
I suggest carrot cake, zucchini
bread, and pumpkin pie.

Jim Davis

Enclosing every thin man, there's
a fat man demanding elbow-room.

Evelyn Waugh

As long as a woman's flesh is
clean and healthy what does it
matter what shape she is?

Ian Fleming

I would rather
be round and jolly
than thin and cross.

Ann Widdecombe

Hunger is the best
sauce in the world.

Cervantes

———◆———

Eat little, sleep sound.

Iranian proverb

———◆———

There is a lot more juice in
grapefruit than meets the eye.

Anonymous

The best way to lose weight is to close your mouth – something very difficult for a politician. Or watch your food – just watch it, don't eat it.

Edward Koch

—◆—

A bagel is a doughnut with the sin removed.

George Rosenbaum

What makes food such a tyranny for women? A man, after all, may in times of crisis, hit the bottle (or another person), but he rarely hits the fridge.

Joanna Trollope

My husband tells me to bulk up if I lose weight – I like that in a man. We often climb into bed with a bowl of cereal and biscuits. It's his idea of heaven.

Nigella Lawson

My husband would fancy me
if I were a beached whale.

Davina McCall

❖

The world is no longer
divided between the fat and
the thin, but between the
very fat and the fairly fat.

Robert Morley

❖

Lots of grapefruit throughout
the day and plenty of virile
young men at night.

Angie Dickinson revealing her diet secrets

I've seen loads of skeletons.
I've never seen one with
'big bones'. Have you?

Sean Meo

I never do any television without
chocolate. Quite often I write
the scripts and I make sure
there are chocolate scenes...
It's amazing I'm so slim!

Dawn French

HUNTING AND GATHERING

Until at least twenty, I cherished the delusion that all food came from Harrods.

Max Hastings

It's bizarre that the produce manager is more important to my children's health than the paediatrician.

Meryl Streep

❧

... the great equaliser where mankind comes to grips with the facts of life like toilet tissue.

Joseph Goldberg on the grocery store

❧

I couldn't foresee that the self-service grocery was going to turn into the supermarket, and then into the superdupermarket.

Russell Baker

They don't know *anything*. You know those name badges they wear? That's for them, not for us.

Sean Meo on people who work in supermarkets

A packet of macaroni as big as a Japanese car is not what I need.

P. J. O'Rourke on king-size packets

Hi-tech tomatoes. Mysterious milk. Super squash. Are we supposed to eat this stuff? Or is it going to eat us?

Anita Manning

I never make a trip to the United
States without visiting a
supermarket. To me they are more
fascinating than any fashion salon.

Wallace Simpson

Food is a human necessity, like
water and air, it should be available.

Pearl Buck

FEELING FRUITY

Watermelon – it's
a good fruit. You
eat, you drink, you
wash your face.

Enrico Caruso

It's difficult to think
anything but pleasant
thoughts while eating
a home-grown tomato.

Lewis Grizzard

If you want to make an apple
pie from scratch, you must
first create the universe.

Carl Sagan

Millions saw the apple fall, but
Newton was the one who asked why.

Bernard M. Baruch

A world without tomatoes is like
a string quartet without violins.

Laurie Colwin

Strawberries are the angels of the earth, innocent and sweet with green leafy wings reaching heavenward.

Jasmine Heiler

* * *

My lord of Ely, when I was last in Holborn I saw good strawberries in your garden there; I do beseech you send for some of them.

William Shakespeare, *Richard III*

Doubtless God could have
made a better berry, but
doubtless God did not.

William Butler on the strawberry

There is greater relish for the
earliest fruit of the season

Marcus Valerius Martialis

Always eat grapes downward – that is, eat the best grapes first; in this way there will be none better left on the bunch, and each grape will seem good down to the last. If you eat the other way, you will not have a good grape in the lot.

Samuel Butler

NICE TO MEAT YOU

Red meat is *not* bad for you. Now blue-green meat, *that's* bad for you!

Tommy Smothers

Vegetables are interesting
but lack a sense of purpose
when unaccompanied by
a good cut of meat.

Fran Lebowitz

Heaven sends us good meat,
but the Devil sends cooks.

David Garrick

I am a great eater of beef and I
believe that does harm to my wit.

William Shakespeare, *Twelfth Night*

My favourite
animal is steak.

Fran Lebowitz

If slaughterhouses had glass walls,
everyone would be a vegetarian.

Paul McCartney

A' shall answer it. Some pigeons,
Davy, a couple of short-legged hens,
a joint of mutton, and any pretty little
tiny kickshaws, tell William cook.

William Shakespeare, *Henry IV Part II*

Persons living entirely on
vegetables are seldom of a
plump and succulent habit.

William Cullen

Ӿ

I think I could eat one of
Bellamy's veal pies.

William Pitt the Younger's last words

CARVING OUT A NICHE

The rule in carving
holds good as to
criticism; never cut
with a knife what you
can cut with a spoon.

Charles Buxton

A lot of Thanksgiving Days
have been ruined by not carving
the turkey in the kitchen.

Kin Hubbard

———•———

Carve a ham as if you were
shaving the face of a friend.

Henri Charpentier

———•———

I just yell at the bird and
hope the meat will fall off.

Jeff Smith

The way you cut
your meat reflects
the way you live.

Confucius

SEASONAL SENSATIONS

Nobody likes turkey.
If they did they
would eat it all year.

Jonathan Miller

Eat plum pudding on Christmas
and avoid losing a friend
before next Christmas.

Old American superstition

———•———

I don't like the turkey, but
I like the bread he ate.

A three-year-old talking about her Christmas dinner

It makes the little ones cry
and the old ones nervous.

Jane Grigson on why 'clever' Christmas
food is not always appreciated

I love Thanksgiving turkey. It's
the only time in Los Angeles
that you see natural breasts.

Arnold Schwarzenegger

A thriving household depends on the use of seasonal produce and the application of common sense.

Olivier de Serres

The man who gives salmon during the winter, I care not what sauce he serves with it, does an injury to himself and his guests.

Ward McAllister, *Society As I Have Found It*

JUST DESSERTS

I want to have a good
body, but not as much
as I want dessert.

Jason Love

I doubt whether
the world holds for
anyone a more soul-
stirring surprise than
the first adventure
with ice cream.

Heywood Broun

Ice cream is exquisite.
What a pity it isn't illegal.

Voltaire

———————

Always serve too much hot
fudge sauce... It makes people
overjoyed... puts them in your debt.

Judith Olney

———————

Custard: a detestable substance
produced by a malevolent conspiracy
of the hen, the cow and the cook.

Ambrose Bierce

Research tells us fourteen out of
any ten individuals likes chocolate.

Sandra Boynton

Without ice cream, there would
be darkness and chaos.

Don Kardong

Seize the moment. Remember
all those women on the *Titanic*
who waved off the dessert cart.

Erma Bombeck

Chocolate is a perfect food,
wholesome as it is delicious,
a beneficent restorer of
exhausted power.

Baron Justus von Liebig

... pastry and plum pudding should be
prohibited by law, from the beginning
of June until the end of September.

Marion Harland

Take away that pudding
~ it has no theme.

Winston Churchill

The dessert, properly prepared, contributes equally to health and comfort; but 'got up' as confectionary too often is, it is not only distasteful to a correct palate, but is deleterious and often actually poisonous.

Eleanor Parkinson, *The Complete Confectioner, Pastry-Cook, and Baker*

Dessert should close the meal gently and not in a pyrotechnic blaze of glory.

Alan Koehler, *Madison Avenue Cook Book*

SAY CHEESE

The poets have been
mysteriously silent on
the subject of cheese.

G. K. Chesterton

A dinner which ends without
cheese is like a beautiful
woman with only one eye.

Jean Anthelme Brillat-Savarin

Cheese is the biscuit of drunkards.

Grimod de La Reynière

How can you be expected
to govern a country that has
246 kinds of cheese?

Charles de Gaulle

Stiltons, with the exception
that they make no noise, are
more trouble than babies.

Stilton cheesemaker

———

Cheese – milk's leap
toward immortality.

Clifton Fadiman

AFTER DINNER MINX: COFFEE, CIGARS AND LIQUEURS

Good cognac is
like a woman.
Do not assault it.
Coddle and warm
it in your hands
before you sip it.

Winston Churchill

Claret is the liquor
for boys; port, for
men; but he who
aspires to be a hero...
must drink brandy.

Samuel Johnson

This Satan's drink [coffee]
is so delicious that it would be
a pity to let the infidels have
exclusive use of it. We shall
cheat Satan by baptising it.

Pope Clement VIII

Coffee: induces wit. Good only
if it comes through Havre. After
a big dinner party it is taken
standing up. Take it without sugar
– very swank: gives the impression
you have lived in the East.

Gustave Flaubert

I respect the pleasure some
people take in the final taste
of a Cognac and a cigar.

Piero Selvaggio

An aged Burgundy runs with
a beardless Port. I cherish
the fancy that Port speaks
sentences of wisdom, Burgundy
sings the inspired Ode.

Ambrose Bierce

Coffee leads men to trifle away their time, scald their chops, and spend their money, all for a little base, black, thick, nasty, bitter, stinking nauseous puddle water.

The Women's Petition Against Coffee of 1674

Only Irish coffee provides in a single glass all four essential food groups: alcohol, caffeine, sugar, and fat.

Alex Levine

I feel the end approaching. Quick, bring me my dessert, coffee and liqueur.

Jean Anthelme Brillat-Savarin's great aunt Pierette

Have you enjoyed this book?
If so, why not write a review
on your favourite website?

Thanks very much for buying
this Summersdale book.

www.summersdale.com